KIDNAPPED!

COULD IT HAPPEN TO YOU?

KIDNAPPED!

BY ELAINE SCOTT

FRANKLIN WATTS / 1989
NEW YORK / LONDON / TORONTO / SYDNEY

Library of Congress Cataloging-in-Publication Data

Scott, Elaine.
Kidnapped! : Could it happen to you? / by Elaine Scott.
p.   cm.
Summary: Discusses the problem of children being kidnapped by
one of their parents, usually parents involved in a divorce,
and suggests ways for children to deal with the problem.
ISBN 0-531-10680-2
1. Kidnapping, Parental — United States — Juvenile literature.
2. Children of divorced parents — United States — Psychology —
Juvenile literature. [1. Kidnapping, Parental.] I. Title.
HV6598.S38   1989
363.8'8'088054 — dc 19   88-39011   CIP   AC

For
Dr. Tena Bolin-Barineau,
with love

KIDNAPPED!

CHAPTER ONE

It's Monday morning and once again, it's time to get ready for school. Your Mom calls you to breakfast, and as you take your place at the table, she puts a bowl of cereal right in front of you. Right in front of you, too, is the carton of milk. You reach for the milk to pour it over your cereal, and your eyes fall on the pictures once again. It seems they're everywhere—on milk cartons, on posters, on pieces of mail—you've even seen some tacked on telephone poles, and mounted on the backs of 18-wheel trucks. Although the faces are different, the message is always the same: Have you seen this child? You peer at the two faces on this particular carton. A boy and a girl, close to your age, look back at you. Below their pictures there is a bit of information about each them, such as their name, age, address, date of birth, and the date they were reported missing. As you read the milk carton, you notice that one of these children has been missing for months; actually (if your arithmetic is right) it's closer to two years. Everyone says you don't look at all like your school picture from last year, and you agree. You've done a lot of growing and changing in the past year. As you study the pictures, you wonder if these children have changed as much as you. If you saw one of the missing children, would you recognize him or her? If you're like most boys and girls, you may think about these questions for a moment or two, but then you finish your cereal and head off to school. The faces on the milk carton are forgotten for a while.

In class that morning, your teacher raps on her desk and asks for everyone's attention. She announces that the parents' organization has arranged to have all the students fingerprinted, then she passes out permission slips which everyone's parents must sign before the fingerprinting can be done. The slips say that the fingerprinting will take place in the school cafeteria this Thursday afternoon. The parents will take the fingerprints home with them. You're not certain you want to be fingerprinted—isn't that something they do to criminals? But to your surprise, after reading the note, your parents decide they want your fingerprints taken.

"Why?" you ask. The faces on the milk carton come to your mind again. And now you remember that the grocery store has put up posters with pictures of missing children on them. And you have seen part of a television show about a boy who was kidnapped and his parents never got him back. Inside, you begin to feel worried—maybe even frightened. Could you be kidnapped? You draw in a deep breath and look at your parents. "Do you think I'm going to be kidnapped?" you finally ask.

It makes you feel better when both of them laugh. "Of course not," they answer. "You're a smart person, and you follow all the safety rules we've given you. Fingerprints are just a good way of identifying people, that's all. When you were born the hospital took your footprints so we could be sure you were you, but those footprints are too small to be any good anymore. We need more grown-up identification. If you ever got lost, we'd want to be able to find you. Fingerprints would help us prove that you are our child."

Your parents seem to think the fingerprinting is a good idea, so you decide it's a good idea, too. And it might be fun to watch a police officer fingerprint the entire 4th grade! You decide not to worry about it. A math test is scheduled for tomorrow, and that's enough to worry about for now! You forget about the fingerprints and begin to practice your division.

Even though your parents laughed and assured you that you wouldn't be kidnapped, the truth of the matter is, all parents worry about their children, and they try to do everything they can to keep them healthy and safe. They worry when they don't brush their teeth. They worry when they don't finish their dinner. They worry when they don't come home on time. They say things like, "Brush your teeth after every meal, so you won't get a cavity." Or "Finish your milk, so you'll have strong bones." Or "Don't talk to strangers, so you won't get kidnapped."

Kidnapped. Strangers. The words themselves are scary. Kidnapped means being taken away by someone, when you don't want to go. You don't have to be taken far away to be kidnapped. You could be kept right in your own city. Stranger is another scary word. Most of us think a stranger is someone we don't know at all, but actually, a stranger is any person whom you, or your parents, don't know very well. When we know people well, we know their names and addresses, we know the names of the other members of their family, we visit in their homes and they come to see us in ours. Those are the people we call friends. Everyone else—even people you see in your neighborhood every day—is still a stranger as far as safety rules are concerned.

Now, that does not mean that everyone you see walking down the street is a dangerous, nasty person. Practically all of the people you see in the grocery store, or walking their dogs, or waiting for a bus at the corner are very nice human beings. They would not hurt a child for anything in the world. Unfortunately, however, there are some people out there who are not so nice, and it's never easy to pick them out from a crowd. The truth is, we simply can't tell whether people are nice or not just by looking at them. And we can't tell what kind of person they are just by talking to them, either.

While their children are growing up, parents say "Don't do this" and "Don't do that" so much that boys and girls often get tired of hearing it—so tired of hearing it that they don't really listen. And because kids are kids, some-times—no matter how many times their parents say it—they don't brush their teeth, and they don't finish their milk. Sometimes, they even talk to strangers, and that is a very big mistake, a much bigger mistake than forgetting to brush their teeth or finish their glass of milk.

As you read this book, you may think to yourself, "Well, I'd never talk to a stranger. I know better."

But what if you've ridden your bicycle to the store for your Mom, and a woman who looks worried comes up to you and asks if you've seen her dog. Be honest. Would you be tempted to at least answer her? The fact is, many people—young people especially—answer questions that are put to them by strangers, especially if they think the people don't look dangerous. They do this even though their parents, teachers, the police—practically everyone—has told them not to speak to strangers. It's not that these children are disobedient. It's just that boys and girls have a hard time ignoring adults who speak to them, because most parents have trained their children to be polite to grown-ups. However, not talking to strangers is a far more important rule to obey than the one about being polite to adults. The lady with the lost dog can ask another adult for help; she shouldn't ask a child she doesn't know. If someone asks you to help them find their dog, cat, car, bicycle, skateboard, ANYTHING—walk away without answering. You don't have to help.

Sometimes a person might offer you a ride to school, or a ride to the nearest candy store, movie theater, or shopping mall. That sounds like a nice thing to do, but it isn't. "Safe" adults never offer children rides, or pieces of candy; they never even speak to children they don't know very well. (Well, maybe a polite adult would say "excuse me" if he stepped on your toes in a crowded elevator, and sometimes older ladies in the grocery store stop to admire a stranger's child, but adults should not start conversations with children they do not know—especially if the children are alone.) Even if you have seen somebody on the street many times, and the person has said "hello" to you and called you by your name every day for two weeks, that person is still a stranger, and you don't have to be polite. You don't have to say "hello" back.

And even if an adult tells you that somebody you love has been hurt and he (or she) will take you to them, DO NOT GO. If your parents were hurt, they would send someone you know very well (probably a member of your family) or a police officer to tell you about it. They would never let a stranger bring you that kind of news.

All of this talk about strangers must be scary, and you may be thinking, "Well, I can't talk to anybody outside of my family and my best friend!" Of course, that's not true. Most adults—even the ones you don't know—are friendly and eager to help a child who needs it and asks for it. But that's the secret—*the child must do the asking.* If someone bothers you near your school, you could return to school and ask your teacher—or any teacher—for help. If you get lost in a store, you can ask a salesperson for help. If something or someone frightens you while you are outside playing, you can ask a neighbor, or a policeman, for help. Firemen, shopkeepers, security guards at banks and stores, mothers taking care of their own children—all of these people would be willing to help a child who asked for it. Remember, *you* can ask for help any time you need it. Adults, however, cannot ask you for help. They must ask other adults.

You can help keep scary things from happening to you by following the safety rules in this book, and by listening to your parents and your teachers. Very, very few children are ever kidnapped or hurt by strangers. The chances are it's never going to happen to you.

CHAPTER TWO

"I'm going to run away from home!"

Ever since families began those words have been shouted (or at least thought!) by children—especially when they're very angry. You may have shouted them yourself at times. It's not unusual to be so angry with your family, or so unhappy with your friends or school, that running away seems to be the best solution to your problem. Many times very small children pack their suitcase with a favorite toy and a candy bar and "run away" only to return home when it starts to get dark or they come to a street they know they cannot cross. Happily, most children who think about running away from their problems do only that—think about it. They don't do it. And many who leave, like the child who could not cross the street, come home when it starts to get dark.

Unfortunately, however, each year there are thousands of youngsters who are so confused and unhappy they actually do run away from home. Most of the children whose pictures you see on the posters and mailers are in this category. They have run away—they have not been kidnapped. Naturally their parents are worried about them and want them to come home, so they arrange to have their children's pictures shown around the country in as many ways as possible. The parents hope that their runaway children will see their pictures and realize how much the parents want them to come home, or they hope someone else will see the pictures and let them know where their children are. It is important for you to realize, when you look at pictures of missing children, that most of these boys and girls are runaways. That is a sad situation, and these children need to be found, but at least you can know that most of them were not kidnapped at all.

When people think of someone being kidnapped they assume the victim was stolen away by a stranger. In the first chapter of this book we talked about how important it is to protect yourself from strangers, since it's impossible to tell if people are nice just by looking or talking to them. It is important to understand the safety rules about strangers, but the truth is, most children who are kidnapped in the United States are not taken by a stranger. Instead, they have been kidnapped by either their mother or their father.

Why would a father steal a child away from his mother? Or why would a mother run away with her children to another part of the country and not let the father know where they had gone? What happens to children whose parents steal them? These are all troubling questions, and none of them have simple answers.

Imagine this. Your bratty little cousin is coming to visit. The last time you saw him, the two of you had an awful fight over your skateboard. He wanted to use it all the time and wasn't willing to share with you. This time in order to keep him from playing with it, you put the skateboard in a place you know he will never discover. That will fix him—surely he'll share next time!

Or perhaps your little sister has made you so angry that you decide to take her favorite doll and hide it. What a great way to get even! That will make her think twice before she picks another fight with you.

Maybe your brother has put his movie money on the shelf. You know he's planning to leave for the theater in just a few minutes. But you're angry because he's not taking you with him, so you take the money. Now he's going to have to beg you for his money if he wants to go to the movies.

At times, all of us take things because we are selfish, like the girl who didn't want to share her skateboard. Or we do things to get even with someone, like the boy who hid his sister's doll. Or we take something so we will have power over someone else, like the person who took the movie money—not to keep it, but to make its owner beg to get it back.

Some of you may have taken something that you shouldn't have without even thinking about it. You see it, you want it, you take it. After you've taken it, you're sorry, but sometimes it's hard to find a way to put it back.

Children aren't the only ones who act impulsively and without thinking. They certainly aren't the only ones who make mistakes. Plenty of adults make all kinds of mistakes. Plenty of adults do things they know are wrong—just like children do. Adults who kidnap their own children make a big mistake, indeed.

Most of these kinds of kidnappings occur when a couple is getting a divorce. Getting a divorce is never easy for parents, and the question of where the children will live is one of the biggest problems of all. Many times each parent wants the child, and yet a child can't live in two places at once. Decisions about custody—who will be in charge of the children—have to be made. Fortunately, most couples can make wise decisions about custody. Together they decide where and with whom the children will live and how often the other parent will see them. They decide how much child support—money to pay for the children's food and clothing and medical expenses—should be paid and who will pay it. As we have said, these are not easy decisions to make, but most parents work hard to find solutions that will be good for their children. And once the decisions have been made, most parents live by them.

However, there are some parents who are so angry, and so hurt, and so confused, and so unhappy about the divorce that they can't make good decisions about who should take care of the children. When parents can't agree about where the children should live, a judge in a courtroom hears both parents' arguments, then the judge makes the decision and gives custody of the children to one or another parent. Sometimes the parent who loses custody takes the children and runs away with them. Why? There are many reasons why adults behave this way. Some are too complicated to explain in this book. But there are some adults who kidnap their own children for some of the same reasons children occasionally take things they shouldn't.

One father couldn't bear the thought of sharing custody of his eight-year-old son with the boy's mother. He ran away with him, and the two of them had to live secretly. The father knew the boy's mother was looking for both of them, but he told his son that his mother was busy with her new job and "didn't have time" to take care of the boy. What this father said was not true, but the young boy had no way of knowing that. This father loved his son selfishly, and he didn't want to share the boy with his mother.

A mother was very angry with her ex-husband. One night, not long after the divorce was final, she packed up everything and moved away, taking her two daughters with her. She didn't leave a note, and no one said good-bye. The father came to see his children and found no one there, and the house was empty. Naturally, he was very worried. The mother wanted to get even with the father for the times the father's behavior had worried her.

Most of the parents who kidnap their children are not bad people—they're just confused, unhappy people. At times, all of us act impulsively without really thinking about the consequences of our actions.

CHAPTER THREE

Perhaps you are thinking, "What's so bad about being taken away by your father or your mother? After all, it's not like going off with someone you don't know. And anyway, how can parents kidnap their own children?"

Of course most parents who divorce don't try to kidnap their children. They work out visitation arrangements, and both parents take turns being with their children. Nevertheless, by 1980 there were enough worried parents looking for their missing children to force the passage of a new law, the federal Parental Kidnapping Prevention Act of 1980. When parents kidnap their children they are breaking the law, and the kidnapping parent can be sent to jail. And even if there is no divorce and no agreement on custody, a parent who takes a child off without telling the other parent and getting their permission is, at the very least, not playing fair. Parents worry about their children, and it simply isn't fair for one parent to take a child away without telling the parent who is left behind.

Sometimes children themselves can help keep a parental kidnapping from happening. Suppose your mother comes into your room one afternoon and suggests that you put a few things into a bag. She tells you that you are going to visit her cousin, who lives in another state. No one has said a word about this trip until this very minute, and you know that you normally don't leave town on such short notice. Perhaps your parents are getting a divorce, or maybe they're just fighting a lot and you're worried that they eventually will get a divorce. The trip doesn't sound like much fun to you. In fact, you're not even sure you want to go, but how do you refuse your own mother? The best thing to do is ask your father for help. Call him at his office, or—if he has already moved out of your house—his home. Tell him about your mother's plans for the trip. If he says it's all right for you to go, then go. If he knows how unhappy you are about going, then perhaps he will talk your mother into changing her mind. If, for some reason, he didn't know about your mother's plans, he can tell her he doesn't want you to go.

This same situation could easily happen the other way around. Maybe the divorce has already happened, and you're visiting your father on one of the weekends he has custody. Suddenly he suggests a quick trip to the mountains to get in a weekend of skiing. You don't have ski clothes with you. In fact, no one has mentioned this trip until now. You think about your mother. She didn't put any heavy sweaters in your suitcase. You feel confused and want to talk to her, but your father says you don't have time to make the call. Try to make the call anyway. It may be perfectly all right with her for you to go on the trip, but she needs to know you are leaving.

Remember, you should never leave town—even with your father or your mother—without saying good-bye to the parent who is left behind. There is always time for a phone call, or a note. If you can't reach the parent you want, then call a neighbor, a relative, or a close friend of the family and tell them that you are leaving. Tell them where you are going and promise to call again after you get there. Ask that person to get in touch with your other parent as soon as they can to let your mom or your dad know you called. It's only fair and right to say good-bye.

Of course, it's hard to make those phone calls if you don't know the telephone numbers. Public phone booths rarely have telephone books. However, even if you don't know the number you want to call, you can punch the "O" for operator. You will have to know the first and last names of the person you want to call, and you may need to know the address, too. If you want to call the office where one of your parents works, you'll have to know the full name of the company they work for. If you have no money for the call, you can tell the operator that you want to call *collect,* which means that the person on the other end of the line will pay the charges. If you are frightened, the telephone operator is a safe adult to talk to. Tell the operator where you are and what you need, and he or she will be able to help you. You can also call the emergency number, 911, if you need help. The operators there are always willing to help boys and girls in trouble, too.

As you can see, it's much easier to make calls if you know the number you want. Memorizing things can be very boring, and most of us really don't like to do it. Some people find it easy to memorize, and others have more trouble doing it. Games like "Concentration" and "I Spy" help people work on their memorizing skills. And there is no doubt that having certain kinds of information memorized can be very handy. In fact, at times that information can be used to help keep us safe. Adults often memorize their driver's license number and the number of the license on their car. That way, they don't have to look it up every time they want to use it. Before you went to school for the first time, you probably memorized your address (including your zip code) and home phone number (including your area code.) By now you have memorized many phone numbers—and most of them probably belong to your friends! But have you memorized the telephone number where your parents work? Do you know the name and address of the companies they work for? You should memorize the telephone number of a relative or a good adult friend, too. You know the name of the school you are attending right now, but do you know the name of the school district? Your teacher can tell you. How about the school you attended before you came to this one. Can you remember its name? Do you know what district it was in?

Don't count on writing this information down in a telephone and address book. Those things are never handy when you need them! Memorizing a few key telephone numbers is the best way to keep you in touch with the people who love you and worry about you when you don't come home on time.

CHAPTER FOUR

Those of you who are reading this book are old enough to understand many things about yourselves, your friends, and your family. When you were younger perhaps you thought all adults knew the answers to everything and no adult ever made a mistake. Now that you are older you can understand that adults—even your parents—sometimes make mistakes. Parents who kidnap their own children make a serious mistake, indeed, and it causes problems for everyone—the parents who take the children, the parents who are wondering where their children have gone, and the children themselves. They have the biggest problems of all.

For one thing, these children may not even be sure they are being kidnapped. After all, as we said in the last chapter, who ever worries about going somewhere with their mother or father? Who even thinks about that as being kidnapped? Children who are very young, say three to seven years old, would not be able to realize what was happening. Even boys and girls who are older would have trouble understanding exactly what was going on. After he was returned to his mother, one ten-year-old boy who had been kidnapped by his father said, "I feel sad that I went along. I guess I should have known better."

Another young girl, who was also taken away by her father, said, "I didn't know I was being taken. I just didn't ask. I went along with it."

The truth of the matter is, most children do "go along" and don't ask questions. They trust their parents. The young man who said, "I guess I should have known better" is wrong; he *couldn't* have known any better. It's not his fault that his father took him away, and he should not feel guilty about going. And the young girl who didn't ask questions should not feel guilty either. Neither of these young people did anything wrong. Some boys and girls simply wouldn't think about questioning their parents. However, all children have the right to ask questions if they don't understand something.

Normal family vacations are usually planned in advance. Everyone in the family knows about the trip and looks forward to it. Even the parent who is not going often talks about the trip with the child and helps the child make plans for it. When a trip is sudden and unexpected, it's okay for children to ask their parents where they are going, why they are going, and when they will be back. Practically all parents will be happy to explain the reasons for a sudden trip—and there are plenty of good ones. Someone in the family could be sick. Maybe a parent won a sweepstakes and all of you are going to Disneyland, who knows? All of us are trained to be polite and not to ask nosy questions, but questions about trips that involve ourselves are not impolite, and they are certainly not nosy. Most parents will happily answer their children's questions, and all parents should let you say good-bye to other members of your family before you go.

When a parent refuses to answer a child's question about where they are going, or won't let the child say good-bye to anyone—especially the parent who is being left behind—there is a possibility that this parent intends to run away with the child. And if that happens, the child and the parent are faced with all kinds of new problems.

Remember, parents who kidnap their own children are often angry and frustrated, and when people are angry and frustrated they do things they might not do otherwise. Perhaps you can recall a time when you took something you shouldn't have taken—borrowing your brother's bike without permission, maybe, or helping yourself to a candy bar at the drug store. As soon as we do something we know is wrong, our first instinct is to cover it up. And usually, we cover it up by telling a lie. Parents who take their children off without permission know they have done something that is wrong. And to cover it up, they, too, will often lie.

Once people start telling lies, their problems get worse. One lie leads to another lie to cover up the first one, and so on. The problems begin to pile up. Eventually the child who is kidnapped has to go to school. Schools keep careful records on each student, and when a student changes schools, the old records are sent to the new school. A kidnapping parent doesn't want the old school to know where the child is, so often the parent will lie to the people at the new school and say the records burned up when the house caught on fire, or something like that. But children's official school records are never in their homes. Schools keep them in a file. Even if your school lets you keep your report card, you can be certain that a copy of it is in your file at the school office. Unless the school burned down, the records will still be there. That's why it's important for the child to remember the name of the last school and the school district it was in—just in case a teacher or a principal asks.

When children have been kidnapped, they often worry about the parent who is left behind. They think about questions like, "Does Mom know where I am?" "Does Dad think I ran away?" "Do they want me back?" Sometimes they work up their courage and ask the parent who took them for answers to these kinds of questions. Unfortunately, the answers the children get are often not the truth.

Sometimes a parent will claim, "Your mother is dead." Or "Your father is a drug addict and we had to leave." Or "Your father (or your mother) doesn't want us anymore." These are hard things to hear. When they get answers like this, children might not want to call home. They are afraid of what they might find out. After all, who wants to be told, "Go away. I don't want you anymore." Sometimes it's easier for these children to believe what they've been told even though, in their hearts, they know it might not be true. And so many of the children who have been kidnapped don't make that important phone call home. And that's too bad, because the parent who is left behind is worrying, and hoping, and searching, and praying that their child will soon be found.

There is another reason why children who are old enough to do it don't get in touch with their other parents. They don't want to get the parent they are living with in trouble. After all, most children love *both* of their parents and they never want to have to choose between them. A parent who takes a child away without permission is usually breaking the law. You know what happens to people who break the law. Very often, they go to jail. A kidnapping parent might even say something like this to a child, "Don't tell anyone about where we lived before. Don't talk about our life before we moved here. It'll be our secret. If anyone finds out that we are running away, I'll go to jail."

Well, no child wants to be responsible for

putting a parent in jail, so that important phone call is not made. And that's a shame, because in truth, most of the parents who snatch their children do *not* go to jail. Instead, when the children are returned, the parents who took them get counseling that helps them handle their feelings of anger and frustration. In fact, everyone involved in the situation—both parents and all the children—can get counseling. Doctors who have special training help each member of the family talk about their angry, sad, hurtful feelings. One or two conversations with the doctor are not enough. The counseling takes a while, but eventually everyone in the family can begin to feel better about themselves and the experiences that they have had.

Up until now we have talked a lot about the feelings of the parents who are involved in this situation. But what about the children? How must they feel? We've already talked about two young people who didn't realize what was happening at the time. There are other children who know what is happening—or at least they have a suspicion—but they are not too bothered by the fact. It might seem like an adventure to be on a secret trip with Mom or Dad. And to be honest, these children might feel a bit flattered, too. They might think to themselves, "Wow! Mom and Dad both want me enough to fight over me!"

These feelings are perfectly natural—everyone likes to be the center of attention once in a while. But those feelings of being special usually don't last. At first the child's life goes on like it did before. The child settles in a new town, goes to a new school, and makes new friends. After a while, however, the excitement begins to wear off. There seem to be a lot of secrets in this new life. These children are told not to talk of their old school, their old town, their old friends. Soon they start to miss the other members of their family—cousins, grandparents, their best friend. It's time for holiday celebrations and these children begin asking questions like, "Why can't we go home for Thanksgiving? We always eat turkey at Grandma's."

As we have said, when people tell a lie, it usually takes more lies to cover up the first one. Taking a child without permission is like telling a lie. It's not an honest way to behave. In answer to the question about Thanksgiving, for example, a parent might say something like, "We don't have the money to go" or "Grandma isn't having the dinner any more." The parent will have answers to questions like these, but sadly, the answer might not be the truth.

As time wears on, and birthdays come and go with no card or present from the other parent, no phone calls or visits, these children might begin to believe something that is the biggest lie of them all. Sometimes they may actually think, "I was bad, and that's why Mom or Dad isn't coming for me." They might remember family rules that they had broken when they lived in their other home. They might remember the day they left home and think of ways they could have stopped the kidnapping from happening—if only they had done something different. Like the ten-year-old boy, they think "I should have known."

The truth is, even if children ignore safety rules, are mean to their little brothers, make bad grades in school or do any of the kinds of things that children do and then wish they hadn't, being snatched away is NEVER their fault. It is ALWAYS completely the fault of the person who takes the child, and that is true whether the person is a parent, a friend, or a stranger.

CHAPTER FIVE

Children who have gone through this experience are sad, confused, and angry—even after they are returned home. They find it hard to trust anyone—even themselves and their own good judgment. Their parents say they love them, but, as one rescued child once said, "Do people have to hurt someone to love them?" And that's exactly how these children feel— hurt inside. They may also feel confused about whether or not they even want to go home— especially if they've been away for a while. To complicate matters further, the children may feel angry toward the parent who was left at home. They may think, "How could Mom or Dad let this terrible thing happen to me?" All of these feelings are perfectly natural—even if they are uncomfortable.

The best way to get rid of uncomfortable feelings is to talk about them. If you're angry at your best friend, you can say "I'm so mad at you I could . . . (fill in your own idea of what you could do!), and I want to tell you all about it." You'd be surprised how "telling all about it" helps get rid of the angry feelings inside. But who do you tell about something like this? For the children who are still with the parent who kidnapped them, there is no special doctor to talk to. A parent can't risk taking the child to one, because the doctor would quickly find out what had happened. So what could children in this situation do? Whom could they turn to for help?

Well, some schools have counselors. A school counselor would be an excellent person to talk to. Counselors are trained to listen well and give good advice. They understand the kinds of feelings young people have, and they are specially trained to talk about those feelings. If there is no counselor at the school, then a favorite teacher or the principal would be happy to listen. And if there's no one at school who seems "just right", then perhaps the child could talk to the parents of a friend. In fact, sometimes it's much easier to talk to a friend's parents than it is your own!

There is no problem that is so awful it cannot be discussed with a trusted adult, but it is often difficult for children to trust any adult after they have been kidnapped. It takes courage to tell someone about a problem, but children can be as brave as many adults—perhaps even braver. As we said at the very beginning of this book, most adults are good, caring people who want to help children, not hurt them. Children are never to blame for kidnapping, and they never caused it to happen. But on the slim chance that it does happen to them, children can do a few things to help themselves get back home.

We've already discussed getting help at school, and you know that anyone—children included—can get help from the police all across the country by just dialing 911. Anyone who calls 911 must be able to tell the operator who they are and what has happened. Then the 911 operator will be able to get help.

Some children might want to call their other parent at home. Or, if that didn't seem like a good idea, they might decide to call a good adult friend or relative. Calls to 911 are free, but calls from a phone booth to a number cost money. However, as we have said, if children have no money, they can still call home

"Collect" by pressing "O" and telling the operator what they want to do. It doesn't cost a quarter to call the operator. All you have to do is pick up the phone and dial "O". The operator is a safe adult who is always ready to help.

Perhaps a child couldn't call home, for some reason. Maybe the phone's been disconnected. Well, there's always the mail. Children old enough to read this book could write a note to their families or friends back home, telling them where they are, including the city and the state. Of course, anyone who writes letters has to know the address to send them to—including the zip code. And a letter or a card has to have a stamp. Stamps can be bought from a machine in practically any grocery store or drug store—the machines take quarters and dimes. If a person didn't know how to operate the machine, any clerk in the store would be glad to help.

There are things that children can do to help themselves, but the very best weapon all of us have to protect ourselves is knowledge of good safety rules. Here is a short list of all of the safety suggestions we've talked about in this book. It might be a good idea to look them over now. If you have any questions about them, ask your mom or dad, or your teacher.

A "stranger" is anyone who is not known very well by your family.

"Strangers" may call you by name; it doesn't matter—if you don't know them very well, they're still strangers. Don't speak to them. Don't answer their questions, either. Walk (or run) away quickly if they try to talk to you or stop you from something you are doing.

Children do not have to be polite to adults they do not know.

Memorize your home telephone number, including your area code. Can you say it to yourself now? Good.

Memorize both your parents' work telephone numbers, including the area code. Can you repeat them? If you can read this book, you can memorize these numbers.

How about your address? Did you remember city, state, and zip code?

Never leave on a trip with one parent without saying good-bye to the parent who isn't going.

Never tell a caller that you're home alone. Say, "My mother (or father) can't come to the phone right now. May I take a message?"

Never give your name, or your family's name, out over the telephone. If someone calls and says, "Who is this?" answer "Whom do you want to speak with?" DON'T say, "This is Sandy or Billy, or Jerome."

Always go to the mall, or the movies, in groups.

Don't take shortcuts; always walk to school and back by the same route.

Most of these safety rules you have heard dozens of times before, and you could probably add many good rules of your own to that list. However, it's a funny thing about learning—we often have to hear things over and over before the information sinks in.

Kidnapping is a serious crime. All parents worry that it could happen to their children—and it could. However, in the United States, children have about a one-in-a-million chance of being stolen by a stranger, so you see, kidnapping isn't likely to happen to you. Nevertheless, even one-in-a-million is one chance too many. And even though most kidnapped children are taken by one of their parents, it's still a very serious situation for everyone in the family. Follow the information in this book—it will help to keep you safe at home.